W
73

Architecture of Truth

Lucien Hervé

Architecture of Truth
The Cistercian Abbey of Le Thoronet

The pictures in this book are witnesses to the truth. Each detail of the building here represents a principle of creative architecture. Architecture as the unending sum of positive gestures. The whole and its details are one.

Stone is thus man's best friend; its necessary sharp edge enforces clarity of outline and roughness of surface; this surface proclaims it stone, not marble; and 'stone' is the finer word.

The way stone is dressed takes into account every fragment of the quarry's yield; economy coupled with skill; its form is always new and always different. Bands, vaulting-stones of arch and vault, ways of setting a window in the thickness of a wall, paving, unsupported pillar and archivolt, roofs and their baked tiles (the same tile endlessly multiplied, male and female – a population of tiles), the shafts of columns, both free-standing and engaged, plinth and capital (but none of these things are there to catch the eye) … such are the words and phrases of architecture. Utter plenitude. Nothing further could add to it.

Light and shade are the loudspeakers of this architecture of truth, tranquillity and strength. Nothing further could add to it.

In these days of 'crude concrete', let us greet, bless and salute, as we go on our way, so wonderful an encounter.

Le Corbusier

Gazing from afar, behold I have seen
approach the power of God …

Amalarius of Metz

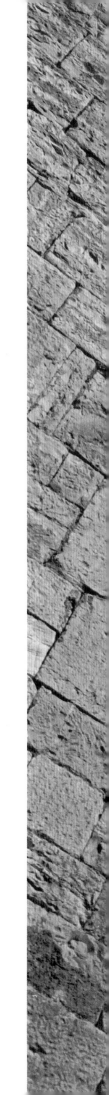

Seven times a day do I praise
Thee because of Thy righteous
judgments.

Psalm 119

Matins

Blessed is he who shall encounter
Thee at daybreak, seated before
the threshold of Thine abode,
who is able to maintain himself
in Thy presence and maintain
himself in it until the evening …
For Thou hidest Thyself in the
shadows, Thou art light and
darkness.

Gilbert of Swineshead

The approach is not by a physical
progression, but by flashes of
succeeding light, and these are
not corporal but spiritual … The
soul must seek light by following
the light.

St Bernard of Clairvaux

Who is she that looketh forth as
the morning, fair as the moon, clear
as the sun, and terrible as an army
with banners?

Song of Solomon 6

Let the shadows give place to
the light, and the night to the
course of the day, let the fault
done in the night-time reel away
at the gift of light …

Father who art in the light, light
of light, light of the day, our songs
break the power of the night, help
those who cry upon Thee.

St Ambrose

Ye also, as lively stones, are
built up a spiritual house, an
holy priesthood.

1 Peter 2

Lauds

Splendour and glory of the
Father, the light out of which light
comes, light of the light and
fountain of light, dawn of the
day's brightness …

May the day go by joyously in
the morning of purity, in the high
noon of faith and without nightfall
upon the spirit.

St Ambrose

Through the tender mercy of
our God; whereby the dayspring
from on high hath visited us,
to give light to them that sit in
darkness and in the shadow of
death, to guide our feet into the
way of peace.

Luke 1

Praise the Lord, O Jerusalem; praise thy God, O Zion. For He hath strengthened the bars of thy gates; He hath blessed thy children within thee.

He maketh peace in thy borders, and filleth thee with the finest of the wheat.

He sendeth forth His commandment upon earth: His word runneth very swiftly.

He giveth snow like wool: He scattereth the hoarfrost like ashes. He casteth forth His ice like morsels: who can stand before His cold?

He sendeth out His word, and melteth them: He causeth His wind to blow, and the waters to flow.

He sheweth His word unto Jacob, His statutes and His judgments unto Israel. He hath not dealt so with any nation: and as for His judgments, they have not known them. Praise ye the Lord.

Psalm 147

More things are learnt in the
woods than from books; trees
and rocks will teach you things
not to be heard elsewhere. You
will see for yourselves that honey
may be gathered from stones
and oil from the hardest rock.

St Bernard of Clairvaux

The roughness of regular
observances and the stone of
discipline frequently bring forth
abundant streams of oil, and
the rigidity of our order like that
of stone makes the soul to feel
the sweetness of prayer.

Gilbert of Swineshead

The voice of the Lord is upon
the waters: the God of glory
thundereth: the Lord is upon
many waters.

The voice of the Lord is powerful;
the voice of the Lord is full of
majesty.

The voice of the Lord breaketh
the cedars; yea, the Lord
breaketh the cedars of Lebanon.

He maketh them also to skip
like a calf; Lebanon and Sirion
like a young unicorn.

The voice of the Lord divideth
the flames of fire.

The voice of the Lord shaketh
the wilderness; the Lord shaketh
the wilderness of Kadesh.

The voice of the Lord maketh the
hinds to calve, and discovereth
the forests: and in His temple
doth every one speak of His glory.

Psalm 29

Faith is not an opinion,
but a certainty.

St Bernard of Clairvaux

He who has put his hand to a great undertaking feels the need for strong nourishment; those who spend their lives working in clay and brick shall make do with the straw of Egypt: we who must travel far have need of stronger nourishment.

St Bernard of Clairvaux

The stone which the builders
refused is become the head
stone of the corner.

This is the Lord's doing; it is
marvellous in our eyes.

Psalm 118

Praise waiteth for Thee, O God, in Zion: and unto Thee shall the vow be performed.

Psalm 65

Your desire is to see, then listen:
hearing is a step towards vision.

St Bernard of Clairvaux

The heavens declare the glory of God; and the firmament sheweth His handywork.

Psalm 19

To be sensible is the property of all things in this world, but their last state is that in which it is written of them that they 'reach from one extremity to another, ordering all things with strength and sweetness'.

Isaac of L'Etoile

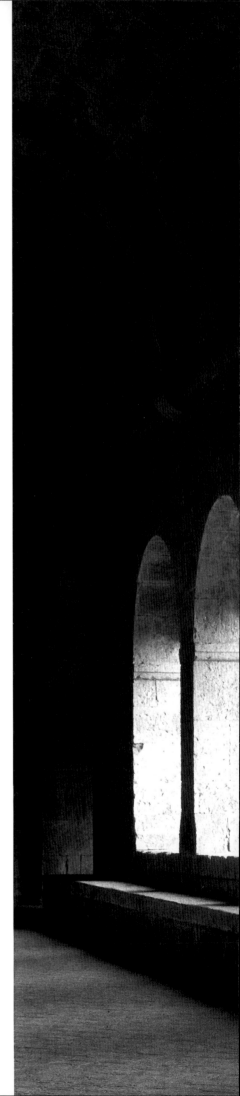

Terce

I will wash mine hands in
innocency: So will I compass
Thine altar, O Lord.

Psalm 26

This silence and this simplicity
are what provide us with the
opportunity for transforming
ourselves, going from light to
light, in the very image of the
Lord whom we contemplate as
though with uncovered face under
the influence of the very spirit of
God … Consecrated to such a
use, does our silence seem to
you to be mere silence and
inertia? Through it we learn and
practise the great art of moving
in a straight line towards God.

Gilbert of Swineshead

However many we are, brought together in the one, at one in the one, made simple by that which is simple, let us, whenever we may, be still with that which is still, sleeping in stillness and resting in it, resting in peace…

Isaac of L'Etoile

That ye ... may be able to comprehend with all saints what is the breadth, and length, and depth, and height.

Ephesians 3

What is God? He is at once the breadth, and length, and depth, and height. Each of these four divine attributes is an object for your contemplation.

St Bernard of Clairvaux

Let those whose care for what is within makes them despise and neglect all that is outward, erect for their own use buildings conceived according to the form of poverty, taking holy simplicity as a model and following the lines laid down by the restraint of their fathers.

Blessed William of St Thierry

In Himself, to speak with exactitude, He is no more wisdom or anything of the kind than He is number or measure or weight … He is nevertheless called Number without number, Measure without measure, Weight without weight, just as He could be called unqualified Wisdom, Justice or Virtue, without feeling or habit of mind being thereby implied … But this would seem to us better expressed if He were called superwisdom, superjustice and so on, being indeed supersubstance. This is not to say what He is, but merely to have something to say … We say what we can when we are speaking of the ineffable, about which in fact nothing can be said: we must either say nothing or else use different words.

Isaac of L'Etoile

It did not enter through the eyes,
since it has no colour; nor by the
ears, since it makes no noise; nor
through the nostrils, since it does
not mingle with the air ... nor by
the throat neither, for it cannot be
eaten nor drunk. Nor did I
discover it by touch, since it is
impalpable ... I rose above myself
and found that the Word was
higher still. Curious to explore,
I went down into my depths and
found in the same way that it was
lower still. I looked outside myself
and saw that it was outside all
that is outside me. I looked within
and saw that it was more inward
than I. And then I recognized as
a truth what I had read: that in It
we have Life, Motion and Being.

St Bernard of Clairvaux

Sext

O high noon, plenitude of heat
and light, fixity of the sun, end
of all shadows, marshes dried up,
pestilence at an end.

O eternal solstice, at which day
no more declines, O noonday
light, O sweetness of spring,
O summer beauty, O fertility of
autumn and, that nothing be left
unspoken, O quietude and
stillness of the winter!

St Bernard of Clairvaux

There are numbered, in this place,
seven aromatic trees which are
nourished by the waters of a
sealed fountain. And the names
by which they are known seem
drawn from a closed book …
There is great glory hidden in this
number and in these names. And
the number Seven, so far as with
God's help we can understand it,
indicates either the spiritual nature
of the graces or their universality.

Gilbert of Swineshead

Nones

It is impossible that man's senses should not be invaded by this heat in the very marrow of his bones which we all know, but that man is worthy of praise, that man is called blessed who crushes such thoughts at birth against the stone. Now, this stone is Christ.

St Jerome

For promotion cometh neither
from the east, nor from the west,
nor from the south. But God is
the judge.

Psalm 75

I am the man that hath seen
affliction by the rod of His wrath.
He hath led me, and brought me
into darkness, but not into light.
Surely against me is He turned;
He turneth His hand against me
all the day. My flesh and my skin
hath He made old: He hath broken
my bones. He hath builded
against me, and compassed me
with gall and travail. He hath set
me in dark places, as they that be
dead of old. He hath hedged me
about, that I cannot get out: He
hath made my chain heavy. Also
when I cry and shout, He shutteth
out my prayer. He hath inclosed
my ways with hewn stone, He
hath made my paths crooked.

Lamentations 3

Why hast Thou then broken down her hedges, so that all they which pass by the way do pluck her?

The boar out of the wood doth waste it, and the wild beast of the field doth devour it.

For I am poor and needy, and my heart is wounded within me. I am gone like the shadow when it declineth: I am tossed up and down as the locust.

My knees are weak through fasting; and my flesh faileth of fatness.

I became also a reproach unto them: when they looked upon me they shaked their heads.

Psalms 80 and 109

Who shall roll us away the stone from the door of the sepulchre?

Who will bring me into the strong city?

Mark 16 and Psalm 60

Vespers

Heavenly city of Jerusalem,
blessed vision of peace
lifting up to the stars
your ramparts of living stones,
you are like a bride encompassed
with a myriad angels,
O strong and fecund spouse
on whom the Father bestows
His glory and the bridegroom
pours out His grace,
most wonderful of queens
at one with Christ in the
beginning, radiant city of Heaven,
by the cunning of the architect
carved with the chisel, struck
out and dressed with the
hammer, your stones dressed
and set together are raised up
to the summit.

Anon., Urbs beata

Such knowledge is too wonderful for me; it is high, I cannot attain unto it.

Whither shall I go from Thy spirit? Or whither shall I flee from Thy presence?

If I ascend up into heaven, Thou art there: if I make my bed in hell, behold, Thou art there.

If I take the wings of the morning, and dwell in the uttermost parts of the sea; even there shall Thy hand lead me, and Thy right hand shall hold me.

If I say, Surely the darkness shall cover me; even the night shall be light about me.

Yea, the darkness hideth not from Thee; but the night shineth as the day: the darkness and the light are both alike to Thee.

Psalm 139

Marvellous Creator of light
Uttering the light of each day
And at the birth of first light
Taking upon Thyself the
world's beginning,

Thou who ordainest that from
daybreak to evening
Shall be called day,
Chaos and darkness fall:
Give ear to prayers mingled
with weeping...

Hear us, kindly Father
And Thou Only who art equal
to the Father
With the Holy Ghost,
our comforter,
Who reign world without end.

Hymns on the Creation

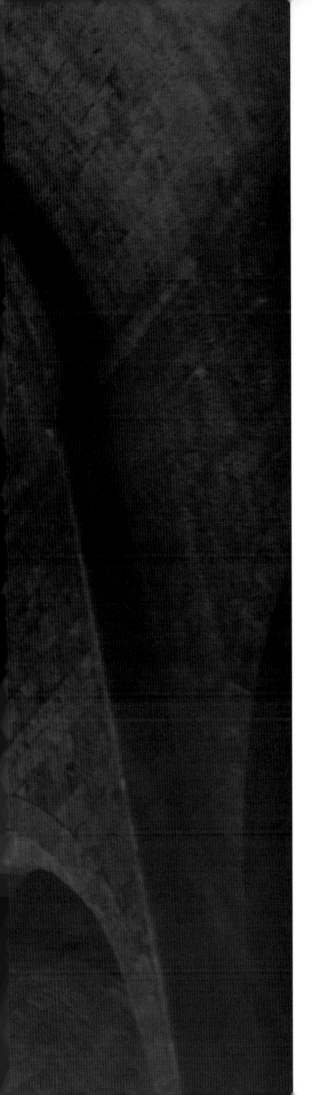

My days are like a shadow that
declineth; and I am withered
like grass.

But Thou, O Lord, shall endure for
ever; and Thy remembrance unto
all generations.

Thou shalt arise, and have mercy
upon Zion for the time to favour
her, yea, the set time is come.

For Thy servants take pleasure
in her stones, and favour the
dust thereof.

Psalm 102

The light I behold is without place;
yet it is infinitely more dazzling
than a mist through which the sun
breaks. This light annihilates for
me all height and length and
breadth; for me, this light is called
the shadow of the living light.

St Hildegard

Compline

I cast my eyes upon the conception and birth of the Virgin and I wonder if, by chance, amid the wonders and novelties without number discovered by one who studies all things attentively, I shall not one day perceive that of which the Prophet speaks to me. Now, what do I see there? Length retracted, height which brings itself down and depth which makes itself level. I see there a light which no longer shines, the word stammering, water thirsty and bread afflicted with hunger.

St Bernard of Clairvaux

Before the light vanishes, we pray you, creator of all things, to hold us in your keeping.

Withhold from us nightmares and phantoms of the night, keep back the enemy that our bodies go unpolluted by him.

St Ambrose

O Lord, rebuke me not in Thine
anger, neither chasten me in Thy
hot displeasure …

For in death there is no
remembrance of Thee: in the
grave who shall give Thee thanks?

Psalm 6

My soul is full of troubles: and my
life draweth nigh unto the grave.
I am counted with them that go
down into the pit: I am as a man
that hath no strength: free among
the dead, like the slain that lie in
the grave, whom Thou remem-
berest no more: and they are cut
off from Thy hand. Thou hast laid
me in the lowest pit, in darkness,
in the deeps.

Psalm 88

The King's banners move forward,
Mysterious shines the Cross
Where life has undergone death
And by his death brought life.

Blessed Venantius Fortunatus

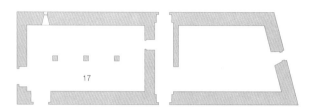

Le Thoronet Abbey

0m 5 10 15 20 25

Christian monastic life began in third-century Egypt. Two hundred years later, the Italian monk St Benedict of Nursia (c.480–543) adapted it to Western culture. He founded the first truly Benedictine monastery at Monte Cassino, Italy, in about 529, establishing the Benedictine Order as a vital and symbolic centre of Western monasticism.[1] This led to a number of subsequent developments, such as the rise of the Cluniac Order in the eleventh century – an early Benedictine reform movement begun in 910 at Cluny, France. In the twelfth and thirteenth centuries, the monastic spirit was gloriously renewed by the Cistercian Order, which had begun at Cîteaux in France, and spread rapidly throughout Europe. However, from the fourteenth century onwards, the Order lost its drive and was plunged into obscurity, suffering through wars, exhausted by the countless quarrels that took place in the Age of Enlightenment, and bravely passing through the French Revolution. It was not until the nineteenth century that the Cistercian Order came back to life, with missions extending to the four corners of the world. Now, its struggles are against widespread religious indifference.

The first Cistercian abbey was founded in 1098 in the woods of Cîteaux, south of Dijon, by St Robert of Molesme (c.1027–1111). He and a group of twenty Benedictine monks had come from Molesme in Champagne, a large and prosperous community, reacting against the superfluous practices of the Cluniac Order there. In this naturally austere new location, Robert and his successors – the Founding Fathers of Cîteaux – sought a simpler life and a more fervent union with God; their aim was to follow a stricter observance of the Rule of St Benedict.[2] This new foundation was part of a trend of contemporary monastic reforms, which also saw the birth of the Carthusian Order in 1084.

Following Abbot Robert's departure,[3] we know of only two monks who took up the abbacy of Cîteaux: St Albéric (d.1109)[4] and the Englishman St Stephen Harding (c.1060– 1134).[5] After a precarious early start, it was during Abbot Stephen's abbacy – between c.1109 and 1134 – that the Cistercian Order truly developed, establishing itself through-out Europe. Bernard of Fontaines (1090–1153),[6] a powerful and influential ecclesiastical figure, entered the Order in 1112, accompanied by a group of novices, and became the founder and Abbot of a daughter house at Clairvaux three years later. In 1174, he was canonized St Bernard of Clairvaux. His arrival was the stepping stone for a spectacular and speedy expansion. Between 1113 and 1115, four daughter houses were established, all of which expanded in turn – La Ferté-sur-Grosne (1113), Pontigny (1114),

Clairvaux and Morimond (1115). Thus, the Cistercian Order grew both in size and geographically. By 1142, the movement had reached Bohemia, just a few years before the foundation of Le Thoronet in Provence, where a monastery had existed since 1136.

Although St Bernard of Clairvaux did not found Cîteaux, he is often regarded as the founder of the 'second generation' of Cistercians. The Order owes much to him: following his death in 1153, there were 350 Cistercian abbeys, 164 of which reported more or less directly to Clairvaux. His work and influence on the Order and the Church is far-reaching and cannot be elaborated here. Nevertheless, one factor is paramount: the importance given to the notion of freedom and sensibility. His doctrine stated that the monks should voluntarily seek to accept the Rule of St Benedict, because this Rule represents God and, moreover, God's law of freedom and love.[7] After having freely accepted the Rule, the monks must follow it without deviation. He also encouraged a transformation that would liberate one's will by directing it towards God. Devotion to God results in the elimination of anything superfluous from the soul and what does remain is not destroyed but transformed. As St Bernard said: 'Whatever is offered to you, if it is not related in any way to your own salvation, reject it!'.[8] The ordered harmony of Cistercian architecture and its unique, systematic approach mirrors this doctrine and reflects such sensibility.

By the end of the thirteenth century, there were over 900 abbeys in Western Europe. The drawback of this significant expansion was that it became difficult to sustain the unity that had singled out the Order for its originality and force. In the thirteenth and fourteenth centuries, the state of Cistercian abbeys varied greatly from one country to another. The effect of the 'commende'[9] was devastating, and relaxation of fervour diminished the importance of the Cistercian Order. By 1400, it had ceased to be prominent, its place being taken by the Dominican and Franciscan Friars. In the fifteenth and sixteenth centuries, reforms lasted only as long as the reformers. The reform of Nicolas II in Cîteaux (1618) or that of Denys l'Argentier in Clairvaux (1620), for example, were both short-lived. More successful were the reforms begun at La Trappe in France in the seventeenth century, led by the Abbot of Rancé (1626–1700), and at Sept-Fons Abbey, led by Dom Eustache de Beaufort (c.1636–1709); those monks accepting these reforms were commonly known as the Trappists or the Reformed Cistercians.

The reformed communities survived the French Revolution (begun in 1789) better than other monasteries, which disappeared during this upheaval. Nevertheless, monks were thrown out of their monasteries, and these were sold off as public property. During the Reign of Terror (1793–4), several monks confessed their faith on the pontoons of Rochefort,[10] while others died of dire poverty or went into exile. After a long journey under the authoritarian and energetic leadership of Dom Augustin de Lestrange (1754–1827),[11] who led the monks from precarious refuges to temporary shelters, those who survived started new communities, returned to France around 1815 and became unified in 1892.[12] Two distinct orders emerged: the Cistercian Order of the Common Observance and the Order of the Strict Observance. Both communities took in many novices up until the Second World War, and today they have expanded to number several thousand monks across the globe.

Through a return to strict asceticism and a life of poverty, the Cistercians sought to follow more closely the Rule of St Benedict and thus recover the ideals of the original Benedictines. In direct contrast to the black habits of the established Benedictines, the Cistercians adopted coarse garments of undyed sheep's wool and hence became known as the 'White Monks'. The Cistercian Order was more broadly based than previous monastic orders, accepting both lay brothers and people from lower social ranks, as well as aristocrats and intellectuals. The monks led an austere and simple life, and their churches were uniform and undecorated. They saw farming as their chief occupation and were also the first to make significant use of lay brothers, 'conversi', who lived in lay quarters at the abbey under a separate discipline. This enabled the monks to devote more time to prayer and spiritual reading. The Cistercians originally intended to follow only the Rule of St Benedict, but in 1118 Abbot Harding formulated new ritual observances and administrative customs. Significantly, he drew up the rule – the 'Carta Caritatis' ('Charter of Love') – which bound all Cistercians to gather at Cîteaux for the annual general chapter and decreed, among other things, that the abbot of a mother house should visit all daughter houses once a year. In addition, the abbots were often recruited for missions unconnected with their vocation; one of them – Eugène III – even became Pope.

The essence of monastic life does not simply reside in silence or poverty; it is about following Christ through prayer and encountering God. This encounter requires a kind of 'stripping away' – a concept that finds its origin in the Bible in the form of Abraham's words, which have always been considered the basis of monastic life: 'Get thee out of thy country, and from thy kindred, and from thy father's house' (Genesis 12:1). A similar teaching can also be found in the many warnings of the prophets, as stated by the Recabites, who are also regarded as ancestors of the monks: 'Neither shall ye build house, nor sow seed, nor plant vineyard, nor have any: but all your days ye shall dwell in tents; that ye may live many days in the land where ye be strangers' (Jeremiah 35:7). This stripping away is not merely an end result, but also a condition and means.

This spirit and life of the Cistercian Order seeks a particular framework and has produced an architecture whose pure simplicity speaks more of the daily existence of its inhabitants than of the period in which it was created. St Benedict initially lived in a cave and cared little about buildings. We have no account of the monastic buildings at Monte Cassino, apart from the fact that the Patriarch lived in a cell and the guest-house was located away from the convent buildings. St Benedict was intent on temperance, quality, humility and respect for what is sacred, and these values guide monastic architecture.

The first Cistercians were committed to measure in all things,[13] which gave rise to their desire to banish anything unnecessary, for 'fundamentally, the unnecessary hides truth'.[14] The Rule of St Benedict stated that monks should 'put quality in everything you do' and like a workshop, the church in which they would 'devote themselves to spiritual art',[15] should be stripped of anything that could distract the craftsman from his work, and nothing should be left that was extraneous to the original intention.[16] From this stem the efficiency, economy and functional concerns that characterize Cistercian architecture. Even the cordons of entablature running from the top of the vaults of Sénanque or of Le Thoronet served as supporting points for erecting the vault.

The issue of poverty also had a strong influence. When considering the long history of the monastic institution, one notices that periods of decadence started with 'a process of temporal realities weighing down',[17] in other words, burdening themselves with worldly possessions, as if to confirm the warning of Isaiah. '… all places that had a thousand stocks worth a thousand silver coins will be covered in thorns and brambles.' (Isaiah 7:12). To be certain that this decadence was a real threat to the Cistercians, one only has to visit the remains of the great Baroque monasteries in central Europe. Like big vessels with perfect proportions, these monasteries have high porches and gaping windows which seem unnecessary simply because of their sheer size.

In the period of greatest expansion (1130–50), the timber structures of the early poverty-stricken years at Cîteaux were replaced by the characteristic large stone churches. The architecture is austere and uniform, and simplicity is strictly maintained – Cistercian churches did not permit visitors or public access and decoration was kept to a minimum. In keeping with the commitment to poverty, Cistercian architecture often draws its inspiration from its locality, both in terms of the surrounding land and its use of indigenous materials. In the twelfth century, the outstanding simplicity and dignity of this architecture culminated in the jewel of Le Thoronet Abbey. The harmony and purity of this stone building is still visible today. As well as giving birth to such architectural splendour, monastic life has brought about monasteries which serve and support the communal and day-to-day life of the monks – the 'living stones' (1 Peter 2) – in their quest for God; the stones, the spaces, and the light are all strong pillars that embody this quest. The organization and architecture of the monastery and its church bring about a spiritual force that help them last.

1 The fruits of St Benedict's monastic experience appear in the Latin Rule of St Benedict. The Rule's 73 chapters, written in a spirit of moderation and common sense, set forth the central ideas of Benedictine Monasticism: in short, that the monks should live communally in an enclosure located far from the rest of the world and should devote their time to attending the divine offices, prayer, spiritual reading and manual work. 2 It was St Benedict of Aniane (c. 745–821) who – during Charlemagne's reign – circulated the Rule of St Benedict, which progressively replaced other rules. 3 St Robert of Molesme, who had already changed communities several times during his long life, promptly returned to Molesme after founding Cîteaux. Documents do not show whether he was forced to return or if he did so of his own free will. 4 St Albéric or Aubry was one of the seven hermits of the forest of Collan, north of Dijon, in the Côte d'Or. He was a co-founder of Molesme Abbey in 1075, later becoming Prior. Also one of the founders of the new monastery at Cîteaux, he became Abbot after St Robert's departure. 5 St Stephen Harding was born in England. In his youth, he entered the Benedictine Abbey of Sherborne. He later left Sherborne, studied in Scotland and France, took a pilgrimage to Rome and established himself at Molesme upon his return. He followed St Robert to Cîteaux, becoming Prior under St Albéric and succeeding him as Abbot on his death. 6 St Bernard was born at Fontaines-les-Dijon in 1090. Aged twenty-one, he was attracted by monastic life; he recruited about thirty members of his family, including five of his brothers, and lived with them for six months in the family house at Châtillon-sur-Seine. He then entered the Abbey of Cîteaux around Easter of 1112, bringing his relatives with him, became founder of Clairvaux in 1115 and Abbot of the same monastery until his death in 1153. 7 Stephen Gilson, 'La théologie mystique de Saint Bernard' (Paris: Editions Vrin, 1934). 8 St Bernard, 'De Consideratione'. 9 Royal appointment of an abbot who does not live in, nor run, the abbey, yet derives an income from it. 10 Yves Blomme, 'Les prêtres déportés sur les pontons de Rochefort' (Saint-Jean d'Angély: Editions Bordessoules, 1994). 11 See August-Hervé Laffay, 'Dom Augustin de Lestrange et l'avenir du monachisme (1754–1827)' (Paris: Cerf, 1998), a glorious epic of the monks who feared neither Robespierre, nor fasting, nor deprivations. The nonconformists sailed for America, England or Spain, thus leading the way for the monastic renewal of the nineteenth century. 12 Dom Sébastien Wyart (1839–1904), former papal 'servant', then monk and Abbot of Monts-des-Cats, and Abbot of Sept-Fons, was instructed by Léon XIII to carry out the unification. 13 Rule of St Benedict, chapters 31, 48 and 70. 14 Frère Jean-Baptiste Auberger, 'L'unanimité cistercienne primitive: mythe ou réalité?' (Achel: Editions Sine Parvulos, 1986), p.282. 15 Rule of St Benedict, chapters 4 and 31. 16 Ibid, chapter 52. 17 Père Adalbert de Voguë, 'La communauté et l'abbé dans la règle de St Benoît' (Editions Desclée de Brower, 1961), p.165.

Afterword

John Pawson

I first made the journey to Le Thoronet some ten years ago, at the insistence of the writer Bruce Chatwin. Although I have returned each year since, the experience of arriving and of walking round the abbey is one which is never dulled by repetition. The setting is breathtaking – Provençal hills, a forested valley, a tributary of the Argens running through. One rounds a corner and, suddenly, there it is – ochre and grey limestone and clay tiles, Le Corbusier's 'architecture of truth, tranquillity and strength'. Le Thoronet remains for me the most beautiful building in the world and the original edition of 'Architecture of Truth' has never been superseded as the most important book on my shelves.

The abbey's architectural and historical significance has long been recognized. When the last seven monks were transferred from Le Thoronet in 1791 and the abbey was due to be sold, the Republic's agent responsible for arranging the sale decreed that the cemetery, chestnut avenue, cloister fountain and church should be designated 'treasures of art and architecture' and therefore 'remain the property of the nation' – arguably one of the first attempts in France to classify a site as an historic monument. More recently, in the nineteenth century, Viollet-le-Duc used Le Thoronet to illustrate the chapter on cloisters in his 'Dictionnaire', surviving examples of split-level medieval cloisters being rare.

Objective historical and architectural merit explains part of Le Thoronet's fascination, but only part. The abbey's continuing architectural relevance exceeds its use as a source of discrete design references or historical detail. There is another less easily defined aspect and it has to do with the way this place forces architects to think, to reflect, to reconsider. The attraction of Le Thoronet is the appeal of a building founded on the notion of simplicity. 'There is no virtue more indispensable for us all … than humble simplicity,' wrote St Bernard of Clairvaux, a twelfth-century monk and key figure in the development of the Cistercian Order and its architectural model. In the sixth century, St Benedict had formulated a Rule which set down a complete approach to monastic life. Monks were to live away from the material distractions of the world in self-sufficient communities. The monastery was to be like an autonomous city, surrounded and defended by a wall of discipline within which the monk would be enclosed until death. Strict observance of the Rule slackened over time. Towards the end of the eleventh century the Cistercian Order was set up by a group of monks who wished to return to the letter of St Benedict's teaching. In the first half of the following century St Bernard of Clairvaux established a comprehensive blueprint for the construction of Cistercian houses which aimed to translate the Rule into architecture.

St Bernard's scheme blended a particular theology with then current developments in building techniques – in stone vaulting, for example – and the prevailing Romanesque style. His aim was an architecture of functional beauty with simple elevations and details. While he conceded that ornamentation might be necessary in a cathedral 'to rouse devotion in a carnal people incapable of spiritual things', he believed that the monk, with his superior spirituality, would only be distracted by material embellishment, the expense of which would also be inappropriate, given his vow of poverty. Crucially, the vow of poverty was not viewed as being incompatible with the highest standards of workmanship.

Le Thoronet was founded by a community of monks in around 1157, only four years after the death of St Bernard. The church, cloisters and monastic buildings were constructed between 1160 and 1190. With only a few minor deviations – some artistic, some practical – the abbey was built to St Bernard's brief. The result is a perfect synthesis of the arts of the master builder and the mason. In keeping with principles of simplicity and economy, local stone – hard limestone – is used throughout the abbey. The result demonstrates how restriction can be turned into strength. As well as offering a perfect context for effects of light and sound, the stone connects the building with its site. We live in a time when architects are able to source materials globally, when trees may be felled in one country, milled in a second and then shipped to a third. The process of design can happen thousands of miles from the proposed site. At Le Thoronet, the walls appear to rise seamlessly from the bedrock; the abbey reminds us of the crucial nature of the interface between a building and its unique site, its stone, its light, its challenges.

With stone used throughout, the relative importance of spaces within the abbey is established through variations in the quality of the cutting and laying of the stone, and through limited carved decoration. In this way a little luxury can be added to the building without theological compromise, the extravagant use of labour being perfectly consistent with St Bernard's brief. The same limestone appears in various guises. In places it is rough cast and relatively crudely fitted together, elsewhere it is cut and jointed so perfectly that its surface feels like alabaster. Wonderful effects are achieved when the rough and the refined meet. Where there are mouldings, these are generally cut into the face of the stone rather than applied onto it – nothing disrupts the impression of smoothness or the purity of line.

The abbey offers a sublime example of what happens when gratuitous visual distraction is removed. The intrinsic beauty of materials is revealed; one sees with incredible clarity. Where there is embellishment – an enriched moulding, a carved capital – every detail is graphically registered. Light also finds its perfect context. Great shards of light carve out spaces in the interior, pools spill across tiled floors and finer, but no less dramatic, threads of light catch in mouldings, tracing semicircular arches, making them appear to be carved not out of stone but etched in solid luminescence. This light is more than a beautiful effect. It symbolizes the physical presence of the divine and it directs attention. In the morning, light is introduced into the church so that one's gaze is drawn always forward, to the curved apse and the altar within it. 'The soul must seek light,' observed St Bernard, 'by following light'. The designer of Le Thoronet (a man of whom, sadly, we know nothing) was shaping more than stones and vaults – he was reinforcing a code of behaviour, confirming a habit of contemplation. Further evidence of this is to be found in the acoustics of the church. A Cistercian monk passes most of each day in silence. The times when he does utter acquire extra significance in consequence. The acoustics at Le Thoronet, with its extraordinarily protracted reverberation, dictates a particular style and discipline of singing. Singers must sing slowly and in perfect unison. Comply, and the effect is ethereally beautiful. Deviate only a little in either respect, and the consequence is acoustic chaos.

Le Thoronet was designed to house spiritual beings as well as physical bodies. It is a highly controlled, ordered, ordering space. When a visitor enters the abbey, he leaves behind the outside world. Having passed through various layers of enclosure, he may believe that he has found something of the outside world again, in the form of the cloister garden, but this is the very heart of St Benedict's enclosed city where different rules apply. In a sense, all architecture creates spaces where different rules apply. Architects are responsible for the ways of living they consciously or unconsciously shape within the spaces they design. Architectural design has consequences which go beyond aesthetics. St Bernard's building programme simply recognized and exploited this.

Nearly a millennium after it was built, Le Thoronet Abbey continues to astonish us with its beauty. For the architect, it offers an entire education. Here is a building which seems to have met fully the practical and spiritual needs of its clients. It conforms to an architectural blueprint, but not at the cost of common sense. It complies with budgetary restrictions all the more significant because they reflect theological principles as well as economic realities. Its construction exploits both the potential of the local stone and the skills of the work force. It relates to its site. In the final assessment, Le Thoronet affords an extraordinary example of the way spirituality and philosophy can become architecture.

John Pawson is an architect and designer. Based in London, he is currently designing a new Cistercian monastery in Bohemia for the monks of the Abbey of Notre-Dame de Sept-Fons. He is the author of 'Minimum' (Phaidon, 1996).

Figures in black refer to pages in the book; all biblical quotations are from the King James Bible. Introduction 7 A leading figure in twentieth-century modern architecture, Le Corbusier (1887–1965) was working on the monastery of Ste Marie-de-la-Tourette at Eveux-sur-L'Arbresle in France (1957–60) when he wrote this short text on Lucien Hervé's photographs. 9 Amalarius of Metz, responses for the first Sunday in Advent. Deacon in Metz in about 840, he compiled a breviary for Louis I, or Louis the Pious, son and successor of Charlemagne. 10–11 Le Thoronet Abbey, seen from the north-west. The Cistercian abbey of Le Thoronet is located near Lorgues, a village fourteen miles south-west of Draguignan in the south of France. It is one of the finest examples of the ascetic architecture of Cîteaux, along with two other abbeys – Sénanque (Vaucluse) and Silvacane (Bouches-du-Rhône), collectively known as the 'Three Sisters of Provence'. The Cistercian monks pursued a strict application of the Rule of St Benedict, which emphasized the importance of a balance between manual labour and prayer, and of a remote location in which to pursue their lifestyle. The architecture of Le Thoronet is characterized by a simple, functional beauty; the pure harmony in the design of the buildings reflects the theological and artistic concerns of the Cistercian Order – volume, light and beautiful stone carvings integrate to achieve a pure and austere harmony, unlike the Benedictine monasteries of Cluny with their use of luxurious materials and ornate decoration. Founded in 1136 at Notre-Dame-de-Florièges – or Florieyes – by Raymond Béranger II, the abbey, a daughter house of Bonnevaux and Mazan, transferred to Le Thoronet around 1157 and was completed in 1190. The abbey originally comprised a church, cloisters and monastic buildings. 12–13 Le Thoronet Abbey, view of church and bell tower from the west. 15 Church, detail of west facade. There are few windows and no buttresses, in keeping with the simple architecture of Cistercian abbeys. 16–17 Detail of the abbey's stonework in the limestone of the region. 18 Armarium or Library, view from the collation gallery. This vaulted room has a semicircular arch and is located next to the church, off the eastern arcade of the cloisters at the southern end of the chapterhouse gallery. The Armarium housed the books used by the monks for their personal meditations and contained books on medicine, geometry, music and astrology, as well as the works of many classical authors, including Aristotle, Ovid, Horace and Plato. The Liturgical books were kept in the sacristy, which can only be reached from the church. 21 Psalm 119:164 (David) – Canonical Hours of the Divine Office (from Latin 'horae canonicae'). The canonical hours are the different parts of the Divine Office – prayers recited daily by priests and those in religious orders, etc. which follow and are named after the different parts of the day. There are seven as David says in Psalm 119: Matins – 3:30 am; Lauds – 6:45 am; Terce – 9:15 am; Sext – 12:15 pm; Nones – 2:15 pm; Vespers – 5:50 pm and Compline – 7:30 pm. (In the Rule of St Benedict which the Cistercians wanted to follow strictly, Lauds originally followed immediately after the night office Matins and Prime was said in the early morning.)

Matins 22 Matins (from Latin 'matutinus' – 'early in the morning, of morning'). The first of the seven canonical hours of prayer, recited at midnight or mid-morning in the Benedictine rule. Originally called Vigiliae until the eleventh century. 23 Church, one of the four apsidal chapels off the north transept. Each chapel is lit by a semicircular-arched window and consists of a short pointed barrel-arched bay with a quarter-sphere vault. 24 Entrance to the armarium and south stairs to the church. 25 Gilbert of Swineshead (d. 1172), quotation from third treatise on asceticism. An Englishman and Cistercian abbot of a monastery in Swineshead in Holland, Lincolnshire. Known as 'Gillebert de Hoilandie' in France. 26 St Bernard of Clairvaux (1090–1153), thirty-first sermon on the 'Song of Songs'. A French churchman, mystic and Doctor of the Church, St Bernard entered the Cistercian abbey of Cîteaux in 1112 and later headed a group sent to found a house at Clairvaux (1115); he is often regarded as the second founder of the Cistercian Order. A powerful religious influence in France, he preached the second crusade (1147–9) and was adviser of the popes, including Eugène III. He was canonized in 1174 and his devotion to the church is evident from his many works, which comprise over 300 sermons, 500 letters and thirteen treatises. 27 Cloisters, western arcade at sunrise. The cloisters form the centre of the monastery. The arcades open onto a central courtyard and garden via a series of semicircular arches divided in half by a large column. A rough-cut capital supports two arches and a tympanum with an oculus. 28 Church, cruciform pillar with engaged columns. 29 Song of Solomon 6:10 (or 'Song of Songs'). The allegorical and spiritual treatment of this poem was largely instituted by St Bernard. 30 Church, from the south aisle; the central nave and north aisle are visible. The church follows the aesthetic principles of Cistercian architecture: with few decorative elements, it is positioned according to the points of the compass and has three wide naves crossed with a projecting transept. The central nave is covered by a pointed barrel vault. 31 St Ambrose (c. 340–397), hymn at Matins on Monday. Arch-bishop of Milan in the fourth century and Doctor of the Church, he was formerly credited with most of the hymns sung at the canonical hours. 32 1 Peter 2:5. 33 Church, north transept from the quire (choir), with staircase leading to the sacristy, the entrance to the monks' dormitory and window of the sacristan bell-ringer's lodging.

Lauds 34 Lauds (from Latin 'laus' – 'praise'). The second of the canonical hours; the morning prayer usually held at sunrise. 35 Church, north transept and apse at sunrise. 36 One of the doorways to the lavabo, which is located off the northern arcade of the cloisters and opposite the refectory entrance, abutting onto the cloister garden and central courtyard. The lavabo is a small hexagonal room with several doors and the cloister fountain inside, which provided water for the monks' everyday use. 37 St Ambrose, hymn at Lauds on Monday. 38 Luke 1:78–79, prophecy of Zacharias, the priest, father of John the Baptist. 39 Cloisters, detail of western arcade at sunrise. 40 Cloister arches, western arcade at sunrise. 41 Psalm 147:12–20, sung at Lauds on Friday. 42–3 Roofs of church and collation gallery from the north. 44 St Bernard, from a letter. 45 View west of church roof from bell tower. The abbey is situated in a valley amid a forest of oak trees. It is near fertile lands and has several streams with a spring. According to the Rule of St Benedict, the abbey should have 'everything necessary – water, a mill, a garden, a bakery and a dispensary – to conduct the various occupations, so that the monks have no need to roam outside, which is in no way beneficial to their souls'. 46 Church apse, detail of arched window. The apse has three windows with decorative insets that accentuate the play of light. 47 Gilbert of Swineshead, twenty-sixth sermon on the 'Song of Songs'. 48 Dormitory (also known as the Monks' Dorter) on the first floor of the monks' building. In the foreground, the stairs lead down to the cloisters; to the right, the windows and doors onto the flat roof over the chapterhouse; to the left, east windows overlooking the cemetery; in the background, the door to the church, stairs leading to the sacristan bell-ringer's lodging (left), the abbot's cell (right) and Treasury walls. 49 Psalm 29:3–9 (David), sung at Lauds on Monday. 50 St Bernard, 'Against the Errors of Abelard'. 51 Chapter-house, stone bench. The chapterhouse is located off the eastern cloisters next to the sacristy in the monks' building. Several steps lead down into this room, its ground floor is lower than the cloisters. The room has a number of windows, six intersecting ribs supported by central columns and stone tiers for seating. The monks met here every morning to read a chapter from the Rule of St Benedict or other religious works. 52 St Bernard, first sermon for the first Sunday after the octave of Epiphany. 53 Cloisters, eastern arcade opening onto the chapterhouse. 54 Psalm 118:22–23. 55 Church, south-east pier of quire. The capitals framing the apse are decorated with crosses. 56 Lavabo, door leading to the cloister garden and central courtyard. 57 Psalm 65:1 (David). 58 St Bernard, source unknown. 59 Church, outer wall of south transept. 60–1 Cloisters, western arcade, angle with refectory wall. 62 Church bell tower, from the south. 63 Psalm 19:1 (David). 64–5 Church bell tower. The Cistercian bell tower was raised over the transept crossing and is supported here by the projecting arch between the transept and quire.

66 Isaac of L'Etoile (d. 1158), sermon 24. Isaac of L'Etoile was an Englishman and abbot of L'Etoile in the diocese of Poitiers in 1147. 67 Collation Gallery, southern arcade of cloisters against church wall. A few steps lead down from the north side aisle of the church to the southern arcade, which is higher than the others and also contains a stone bench.

Terce 68 Terce (from Latin 'tertius' – 'third'). The third of the seven canonical hours, about 9:00 am. 69 Carving of capital at southern end of west cloister walk. 70 Lavabo, cloister fountain. The cloister fountain provided water for the monks' everyday use. 71 Psalm 26:6 (David). 72–3 Monks' Dormitory, detail of stonework above the doorway to the abbot's cell. 74 Gilbert of Swineshead, letter to a certain Adam. 75 Church, exterior window from the east. 76 Isaac of L'Etoile, sermon 21. 77 Roof of the monks' building and bell tower platform. 78 Church, west facade and south door leading to south aisle. There is little decoration and no central door, in keeping with the rules of Cistercian architecture. Cistercian abbeys were not designed for public worship; they were quiet, contemplative spaces reserved for monks, unlike secular churches which were ornate and designed to welcome and edify believers. 79 Ephesians 3:17–18 (Paul). 80 St Bernard, 'De Consideratione'. 81 Church facade, from the south-west. 82 Church and southern arcade of cloisters from platform outside monks' dormitory. 83 William of St Thierry, letter to the Brethren of Mont-Dieu. William of St Thierry was a close friend and the first biographer of St Bernard. A nobleman from Liège, he studied under St Anselm, then entered the Benedictine abbey of St Nicaise at Rheims and in 1119 was nominated abbot of St Thierry, which he left in 1135 for the Cistercian abbey of Signy. This letter to the Carthusians of Mont-Dieu, known as the Golden Letter, was his spiritual testament. 84–5 Cloisters, central courtyard and lavabo from the bell tower. 86 South pier and carvings on chapterhouse capital from the cloisters, eastern arcade. The carved forms are probably pine cones; one of the few figurative details carved in the abbey's stonework. 87 Isaac of L'Etoile, sermon 22. 88–9 Patches of light from the sun's rays shining through the oculi of the cloister arches (western arcade). 90 St Bernard, sermon 74 on the 'Song of Songs'. 91 Cloister arches, north end of western arcade.

Sext 92 Sext (from Latin 'sexta hora' – 'the sixth hour'). The fourth canonical hour or the sixth hour of the day at noon. 93 Chapterhouse, detail of vaulted roof at northern end of gallery. 94 Lay Brothers' Dormitory, internal wall at midday. The lay brothers' building and the cellarer's grange are located off the western arcade of the cloisters, accessible through a small courtyard. 95 St Bernard, sermon 33 on the 'Song of Songs'. 96–7 Church roof and surrounding countryside from the bell tower platform. 98 Cloister garden with collation gallery in the background and the eastern arcade of the cloisters or chapterhouse walk on the left. 99 Gilbert of Swineshead, extract from the 'The Seven Aromatic Trees in the Garden of Christ' from sermon 36 on the 'Song of Songs'.

Nones 100 Nones (from Latin 'nona hora' – 'the ninth hour'). The fifth of the canonical hours or the ninth hour of the day, about 3:00 pm. 101 Cloister arches at southern end of chapterhouse walk, from the collation gallery. 102 Oculus of cloister arch. 103 St Jerome (c. 340–420), 'De Virginitate'. A Christian scholar, Father of the Church and Doctor of the Church, his most famous work was the Vulgate translation of the Bible (the official Latin version of the Roman Catholic Church), which was prepared in c. 383–405 at the request of Pope St Damasus 1. 104 Psalm 75:6–7 (Asaph), sung at Nones on Friday. 105 Cloisters, detail of capital and oculus. 106 Window in lay brothers' building. 107 Lamentations 3:1–9 (Jeremiah). 108 Psalms 80:12–13 (Asaph) and 109:22–25 (David), sung at Nones on Saturday. 109 Walls and doorway of lay brothers' building. To the right, the west wall of the cellarer's grange where a wide door and arched openings once existed. An oil press, wine-vats and a baker's oven were kept in the cellarer's grange. 110 Monks' Dormitory, doorway to church. The stairs on the left lead to the sacristan's lodging. 111 Mark 16:3 and Psalm 60:9 (David).

Vespers 112 Vespers (from Latin 'vesperus' – 'evening'). The sixth canonical hour, held in the early evening at sunset. Also known as Evensong. 113 Church, interior with oculus of west facade at sunset. 114 Anon., 'Urbs beata' – seventh-century hymn for the dedication of churches. 115 Church, south door, oculus and window of west facade at sunset. 116 Church, detail of Cistercian plinth. 117 Psalm 139:6–12 (David), sung at Vespers on Friday. 118–9 Northern transept of church from the south, with one of the apsidal chapels on right. 120 Church, east end of nave at sunset. 121 Hymns on the Creation, sung at Vespers and attributed to St Ambrose. 122 Church nave, west end at sunset. 123 Psalm 102: 11–14 (prayer of an afflicted man), fifth penitential psalm. 124 St Hildegard (1098–1179), extract from 'The Shadow of the Living Light'. A mystical writer and German abbess, first of Disibodenberg and subsequently of Bingen, which she founded. She has never been canonized, though proclaimed a saint by her followers. 125 Cloisters, eastern arcade or chapterhouse walk at sunset. 126–7 Cloisters, detail of eastern arcade with steps leading to the cloister garden.

Compline 128 Compline (from Latin 'hora completa' – 'the completed hour'). The last of the canonical hours, said about 8:00 or 9:00 pm and completing the series of daily prayers or hours. 129 Cloisters at sunset, view from the chapterhouse. 130 Cloisters at sunset, view through chapterhouse doorway. 131 St Bernard, second homily on the glories of the Blessed Virgin. 132 Chapterhouse, detail of carving on the north pillar. 133 St Ambrose, hymn at Compline. 134–5 Monks' Dormitory, west windows at sunset. 136 Chapterhouse, detail of vaulting. 137 Psalm 6:1 and 5 (David), sung at Compline on Monday. 138 Psalm 88:3–6 (Sons of Korah), sung at Compline on Saturday. 139 West gate of monastery precinct. 140 Cloister arch at sunrise. 141 St Venantius Fortunatus (530–609), from the hymn 'Vexilla Regis prodeunt' which was sung on Good Friday in the Roman Catholic Church. A priest in Gaul and bishop of Poitiers, he was the last of the Gallic Latin poets. 142–3 Monks' Dormitory at night. 144–5 Plan of the monastic buildings of Le Thoronet Abbey, as they were in the thirteenth century. Drawn by Stéphane Orsolini.

Lucien Hervé: Biography

Lucien Hervé (né Laszlo Elkan) was born in 1910 in Hungary. He studied drawing in Vienna before moving to Paris in 1929, where he worked as a fashion stylist before taking up photography. During the Second World War, he was made a prisoner of war in Germany; he later escaped to Grenoble in 1941 where he joined the Resistance and assumed the name Lucien Hervé. After the war he became friends with the late Father Couturier, editor of the magazine 'L'Art Sacré'. He introduced Hervé to Henri Matisse, whom Hervé photographed. He also persuaded Hervé to document Le Corbusier's Unité d'Habitation (1947–52) in Marseilles, which marked the beginning of a long collaboration and friendship with the architect. Henceforth, Hervé dedicated his time to photographing twentieth-century architecture, in particular the buildings of Corbusier, although in parallel he took many artists' portraits and pictures of everyday life. Also a keen painter, Hervé is known for the unique style and pioneering nature of his photography – a tendency towards abstraction and strong geometrical compositions. His work has been exhibited since the 1950s, including at the Galerie Camera Obscura, Paris, the Vitra Design Museum, Weil am Rhein, Michael Hoppen Gallery, London, Gallery 292, New York and Gallery Taisei, Tokyo. It is also featured in collections worldwide, including The Getty Center, Los Angeles, the Victoria and Albert Museum, London and Bibliothèque Nationale, Paris. Lucien Hervé lives in Paris.

Dedicated to the late Father Couturier

Lucien Hervé's photographs of Le Thoronet Abbey
were previously published in French by Arthaud
under the title 'La Plus Grande Aventure du
monde' (1956) and in English as 'Architecture of
Truth' by Thames and Hudson and George Braziller
(1957). This book is a newly created volume that
presents these classic photographs alongside
quotations and new texts in an original design.

Phaidon Press Limited
Regent's Wharf
All Saints Street
London N1 9PA

Phaidon Press Inc.
180 Varick Street
New York, NY 10014

www.phaidon.com

First published 2001
© 2001 Phaidon Press Limited
Photographs © Lucien Hervé
Le Corbusier text © Fondation Le Corbusier

ISBN 0 7148 4003 3

A CIP catalogue record for this book is available
from the British Library

Designed by John Pawson and William Hall

Printed in China